REAL ESTATE RICHES:

NO COLLEGE REQUIRED

How Anyone Can Make a Fortune
Investing In Real Estate

By

Dr. Steve Joel Moffett, Sr.

POWER THINKING PRESS

San Francisco   -   Dallas   -   New York

YOU MAY CONTACT THE AUTHOR:
Dr. Steve Joel Moffett, Sr.
8250 Calvine Road Suite C-117
Sacramento, CA 95828
Mobile Phone: 916-895-6434

www.revstevemoffett.org
drmoffett@revstevemoffett.org

Dedication

First I give honor, and respect to my Lord and Savior Jesus Christ. And recognition to my paternal Grandfather (the late) Rev. Ezra Moffett and my grandmother (the late) Annie Mae Duckworth - Moffett. My Grandfather Ezra who we affectionately called "Paw Paw" was one of the organizers and founders of Rock Hill Missionary Baptist Church, now known as Blue Mountain Baptist Church in Baysprings, Mississippi, the church has a cemetery where their remains rest. Also, to my maternal Grandfather (the late) John Ellis Jr. and my grandmother (the late) Viola McGee – Ellis who were lifelong members of Warren Hill Methodist Church, in Louin, Mississippi, the church has a cemetery where their remains rest. And to my mother Mary Etta Jones who was primarily responsible for my educational achievements.

Special Acknowledgement

Willie Lee Ellis

November 14th 1928 – August 29th, 2013

To my Uncle (the late) **Mr. Willie Lee Ellis** who was my first employer at age 12, and my father in entrepreneurship. Not only did he employ me, he employed and supported many members of our family and countless others in his business. He was my first work and business mentor, who taught me about investing and business. He helped me pick and he personally purchased my first publicly traded stock (American Home Industries). He also taught me to work smart and hard, and gave me my start as an investor. Without his help and encouragement my life could have never been as rich and exciting as it has been. May God continue to bless you in your Heavenly Estate. Thank You!

TABLE OF CONTENTS

INTRODUCTION

You may have observed other people who are wealthy and rich, who live in the best homes, drive the best cars, eat in the finest restaurants, and wear designer cloths. And you may have wondered, and asked yourself the questions. What have they got, that I don't have? And what do they know that I don't know? You may wonder to yourself, why you work so hard, and it seems like you don't really get anywhere. You may wonder why it seems like you cannot progress and move ahead. You may feel at times that you are standing still. Your neighbors seem to have more money, more free time, take more vacations and have a better quality of life than your family. Have you ever wanted to know the key to their prosperity? Did you ever think that they had some information that others have, that you don't have? Are you lacking some information you need for true success? You don't have to wonder and question yourself any longer. You definitely don't have to miss out on having your own life of prosperity.

You are correct in your assumption that there are secrets to prosperity that some people possess that other people never get. In fact these secrets of success most of the masses of people in the U.S. will never understand. You too can be one of the people that have wealth instead of one of the people that struggles in life. The secret is that much of the great "American Dream" is grounded in real estate ownership, and the benefits that are attached to real estate possession. There are many positive benefits of real estate ownership such as tax advantages, elevated social status, and property appreciation to name a few. However; the main benefit of real estate ownership is the large amounts of money that can be accumulated by anyone who owns, trades, buys or sells real estate.

It is a well-known fact that there are more "self-made millionaires" from the real estate industry, than any other industry in the United States. The new money real estate millionaires definitely by far outnumber all other categories of new money millionaires in the United States. Real estate has made more new money millionaires that than stocks, bonds, oil, gas, retail, manufacturing, food service, hospitality, technology and all other industries combined. It is also true; that the profits from real estate are so enormous that even people who possess average intelligence can succeed. And even those without a college degree, can create and amass a personal fortune in real estate. I once had a client make a lot of money accidently in a real estate purchase and sale transaction. The client purchased a California suburban residence to live in for $215,000.00 with $10,000.00 down payment and assumed the property that had 3 mortgages on it. Two years later the client was forced to sell the house after making a $50,000.00 miscalculation and paying off the third mortgage, and then finding she had to move out of town anyway. To her surprise the house sold for $485,000 and the client made an astronomical $205,000.00 profit by accident on the forced sale. Also, a well-known real estate mogul and entrepreneur, who is frequently seen on television, was heavily invested in the Texas real estate market when it crashed in the 80's. He made 258 million dollars when his development corporation went bankrupt. The investor considered this a business failure, not because of the bankruptcy, but because he could have made over 1.5 billion dollars if the market had not crashed in the middle of his housing developments. Just think if people can have huge, setbacks and make stupid mistakes and still make a lot of money in a real estate transaction, maybe it is the business for you. I am not saying for a moment that you are stupid. What I am saying is that if you are not stupid, you should be very successful in the industry. I started developing homes when I discovered just how much money developers earned building new homes. You can be "not so smart" and still make a lot of money, because the profit potential of real estate transactions are so tremendous. If you sold television sets for $300.00, with a $100.00 profit built in, you would have to sell 500 (five hundred) televisions to make $50,000.00. In a simple real estate flip transaction you could make $50,000.00

on only 1 (one) small transaction. Real estate agents, brokers, developers, financiers, traders, and landlords make billions of dollars annually off the real estate market, while most people just sit on the side lines and pay rent or buy just one house to live in. You could make a fortune also, if you knew the secrets to making money. Now you can have all the information you need to be successful in real estate investments.   I will reveal many of the secrets real estate investors use within the pages of this book. This book makes these secrets to real estate success available to all. Everyone that is willing to read and study the concepts illustrated in this book, and write some offers can make a lot of money. As an educator I certainly don't want to represent that education is not important, neither do I want to discourage anyone from going to institutions of higher learning. College will help, but there are many examples in our society of rich successful men and women, who never attended a college or university. These people achieved greatness and wealth, some of them without a high school diploma. Education is a good insurance policy. If you have or seek higher education, it will not spoil these opportunities for you, it will only enhance them. These secrets will work for anyone that diligently applies them. You also, can be successful and can live in the best homes, drive the best cars, eat the best food, and amass a fortune. I remember seeing a Rolls Royce with the license plate reading "U Can Too". And I want to let you know, that you can be successful as well in real estate. Success with only ordinary intelligence and skill, with no other specialized training. This book will offer you a part time or full time career or hobby that will make you rich without ever setting foot in a classroom. Like that Rolls Royce owner wanted everyone else to know. You don't have to live in envy and jealousy of the accomplishments of others. You too can walk in the shoes and follow the path that many millionaires have already treaded. You can have success, status and make hundreds of thousands of dollars and maybe even millions. Just keep an open mind, believe in yourself and you will succeed. Investment success happened for me and I believe it will happen for you.

If the vision is great, then the facts don't matter.

(Author Unknown)

Free!

LAND

CHAPTER 1

HOW TO GET FREE LAND

...This first technique is the simplest of all investment strategies, and can help you acquire land at no cost. It is a wonder why it is not used more often to acquire free real estate. It is so simple, that it is easy to overlook. This strategy can be used over and over again to acquire real estate with very little effort, and no real expense. I first saw this strategy when it was used by a Chevrolet auto-dealer I was working for. He used the technic to purchase a 5 acre piece of land for his dealership at a price of $150,000.00. He then split the lot into two 2 ½ acre parcels. He later sold one 2½ acres parcel to a bank that wanted to establish a new branch in that area for the price of $150,000.00. So he effectively got his property for free. The property turned out to be one of the most expensive pieces of real estate ever in the history of San Jose, California. The property many years later sold to a mall developer when the dealership moved down the street to a new location. After his demise the auto-dealers family sold the dealership parcel to that mall developer for over 352 million. You too can use the same technique to get free land. All you have to do is buy a parcel of land, which can be split into two parcels. You then sell one half of the property for the amount of the original purchase price, and keep the parcel that remains for free. Alternatively, you could sell both parcels after the split and double the amount you paid for the original undivided parcel. For example you can buy a 1 acre piece of land for $50,000.00 and literally take a slide ruler and divide it into two 1/2 acres parcels. Then place both parcels up for sale at $50,000.00 each parcel. If you decide to sell both, you will then have a $100,000.00 return, and a $50,000.00 profit, but no land. You don't need a large down payment or $50,000.00 in cash to pay for the land. You can put zero down, $500.00 down, $5,000.00 down or whatever you can get a property seller to agree to. Just remember that everything is negotiable in business. The down payment interest rate and the length of any contract are all negotiable. Also, instead of paying cash, you can bank finance the property and make payments until one or both of the parcels sells. If either one sells for the $50,000.00 asking price you can pay off the loan and keep the other half acre of the parcel without the need to make further payments. This initial sale will pay off all existing loans on the property you keep. When this happens you will not only get your down payment back, but you will also be able to increase your cash flow because you will no longer be obligated to make monthly payments. You can speed up the sale of your mini-development by making a small investment, and putting up a real estate sign with a professional artist model of the home you are planning on the lot you are keeping. Putting up a professional high quality painting of future development is highly recommended and should pay great dividends. Even though you have not built a structure yet, the sign with a picture of the coming development will add value to both properties. Like they say; a picture is worth a thousand words. In real estate a development concept picture can be worth tens of thousands of dollars. Anything you do to improve the property that you are keeping will enhance the property you are selling. All improvements will increase the value of both properties in the mind of buyers. Improvements such as bringing water, electricity, natural gas, or a paved road will make both parcels appreciate quickly. Even though all improvements themselves have costs associated with them. It is more cost effective to bring water, electric, sewer or natural gas to your keeper property. But, if you can bring these services also to the property you are selling at the same time, this will enhance the value of both properties immensely. Remember the more you develop the property the quicker you will get your money out of it. You will eventually get your money anyway, but it is nice when you can take a few small steps to turn your property and money over quicker. You don't have to do anything really expensive it could be as simple as cleaning up the property. You can also increase the value of the property and increase the desirability of the property by getting a building permit for a custom house pre-approved with the city or county. Some developers submit several different floor plans for one house footprint. They also sometimes submit a blueprint with same floor plan, but different exterior finishes.

Sometimes they get building permits for 2-3 different kinds of houses for a single lot, to give the buyers pre-approved choices of various types of houses to build. The buyer could then maybe choose to build a split level, ranch, or cottage. Other plans options might be a 2 bedroom plan, a 3 bedroom plan, or a 4 bedroom plan, the variations are endless. These permits assure the buyer that they can build on the lot, because the seller has already done important development work to verify that the project is feasible and allowable. Getting these building permits in advance of the sale of the land is a powerful motivator for potential buyers. You could alternatively build a garage, barn, dig a well, put in a driveway, or put in attractive shrubs and trees which are also desirable improvements. In most states the cities and county building departments have special provisions for a simple split, and they make this type of split very easy for you. If you are only going to do a simple split, the paperwork and expense is usually minimal, because you avoid the stringent rules that apply to major subdivisions. You probably won't need an engineer, zoning approval, nor have any expensive obstacles faced by major sub dividers by doing a simple 2 for 1 split. If you are trying to create more than two parcels from one parcel you will probably need to get professional engineering help, and it will be more costly. For a major subdivision there will be many other rules and requirement for the split. But using this simple 2 for 1 subdivision split technique you will not need to spend a lot of money, or invest a lot of time. Just divide the property in half and file the new split parcel map with the city or county. After the split the building department will replace the one property APN (Assessor Parcel Number) with two APN's then you can list the parcel(s) for sale separately and individually.

This strategy can also work to get you a free house, by buying a split-able lot and building two houses. After they are built you sell one home, and use the proceeds to pay off the other home. Then you can live in the remaining home without a mortgage, freeing you from monthly payments. The primary major expense for every citizen is housing.

Here is an example: If you bought a buildable lot for $50,000.00 and split it. And after the split you took out a construction loan for $300,000.00 to build two homes. And after construction if you sold one of the homes for $350,000.00, you would have no debt on the remaining home. Wouldn't it be nice to live in a beautiful new home with no mortgage? This would be a big step toward financial independence. Before you build, check with an appraiser to make sure the house you are building is going to appraise for $350,000.00 or whatever your breakeven point is. This is just the basics on a 2 for 1 split. I am sure will come up with ideas to improve it.

CHAPTER 2

CONTROL THOUSANDS FOR PENNIES:

WITH OPTION CONTRACTS

...The beauty of option contracts is that it does not require a lot of money to control an expensive piece of real estate. And if you control real estate using an option contract instead of buying it, you won't have to make mortgage payments, insurance payments or do costly upkeep. The property still belongs to the seller, because you are not the buyer, you are just the potential buyer. As the potential buyer you are not responsible for cost and upkeep unless specified in your option contract. If you don't use an option contract, buy a property outright, you are required to put down 10% - 25%. You will also be responsible and committed to make mortgage payments at 3% - 8% interest, plus pay for insurance and maintenance. Also, you will usually have a very short due diligence period like 30 days. This is an expensive proposition which could run into the tens of thousands of dollars. With and option contract you can tie property up while you decide how to best capitalize on the purchase. Option contracts help you avoid expensive mistakes, such as making a purchase and finding that the transaction you had in mind is impractical. Option contracts effectively take the property off the market without the need for a large cash outlay, and commitment of your credit and other resources. You can also profit by selling your option to purchase to a third party buyer or investor, without exercising the option to buy the property yourself. If you found a property for sale which was a 3 bedroom 2 bath home for $100,000.00 and you purchased it because you think you could flip the house quickly for $150,000.00 with a $5,000.00 facelift. Acquisition costs for an outright purchase would take about 10% down or $10,000.00 cash, escrow fees and insurance of approximately $3,000.00 and monthly payments of about $700.00. If you are buying any property on speculation of resale, the cost of holding property longer than necessary is counterproductive. In this particular scenario holding the property longer than necessary could cost you approximately $35,000.00. Even if you sell the property for $150,000.00 for the cost of acquisition, extended hold time, and realtor's commission costs to sell would cut deeply into your profit. In some investment situations not using an option contract would wipe out all or most of the profits of any potential resale. This extra expense would make the transaction impractical. Without using an option contract you would only have a profit of $15,000.00 if everything went perfectly. If anything goes wrong, like you find you will have to keep the property even longer than you expected, or you have an unexpected expensive repair cost. The additional repair and extra months of mortgage payments could wipe out your profit altogether. You could end up making nothing or worse losing money on the deal. However, if you use an option contract to control the property, you can make more money, and create a greater cushion to protect yourself from unexpected expenses and costs. Using this same scenario with an option contract, you find a 3 bedroom 2 bath home for $100,000.00 with the potential sale price of $150,000.00 after you spend $5,000.00 (carpets and paints and yard work) you would have a potential $45,000.00 profit. You tender an option contract that says the seller agrees to sell to you the buyer the 3 bed 2 bath home for $100,000.00 for option money of $500.00 - $1,500.00 dollars, and give yourself 90 days to do your due diligence on the property. The option contract should state that the option is transferable to a third party. So, if you decide that the profit is there, but you don't want to do the work, you can decide not to exercise the option yourself, and just sell it. You could just find an investor, show them the profit potential of $45,000.00 and sell the option for $5,000.00 and let the investor make $40,000.00 instead. If an option contract is written correctly it can be listed on the MLS (Multiple Listing Service). The MLS is the marketing service used by realtors and agents to list properties. Selling the option to another investor who has more cash and credit resources lets you profit, just not as much. This may be more advantageous, because you are then free to work on other more lucrative projects. If you paid $500.00 for an option, you can potentially sell the option contract to another investor for $5,000.00 and still make 1000% on your money. In other scenarios you could even make more depending on the transaction and profit potential of the property. If you see a much greater profit in the property than you first expected, then you could keep the option yourself. For example you find that this particular property could re-sell for $200,000.00, you could decide to exercise the option yourself, by getting a regular bank loan and keep the entire $100,000.00 profit. That is why they call it an option contract; you have the option, but are not required to execute your option. Alternatively, you could still also partner with another investor who has more money and credit and share the $100,000.00 profit. The main benefit of using option contracts is that if you find out that the property is not worth what you thought it was worth, or that you could lose money, you can choose to forfeit the option money, and not exercise your option at all. This way, all you lose is the small amount you paid for the option, plus any minor expenses for investigating the property. If you purchase without an option contract, once your offer is accepted you have no option, you must purchase the property or you could be sued in court, and forced to perform the contract, or pay for the seller's losses, as a penalty for you not going through with the purchase contract.

Option contracts can be a useful tool in creating real estate wealth, because of the way they can limit your exposure to losses, but hold the transaction in suspense until you can come up with the best strategy to maximize profit potential.

You should study some sample option contracts found on the internet, and then write a few sample contracts, before making an offer. You can also get a sample option contract from a local real estate agent or realtors association. Alternatively, you could have an agent or broker represent you and they could write your option contract for you. The agent or broker will usually write the option contract for free or small fee on the strength that you may exercise the option. They will then earn a commission on the purchase contract subsequent to you exercising the option. This is of course their motivation for writing the option contract for little or no cost.

Remember that sellers like option contracts because the option money is money that can be spent right away. Option money never needs to be refunded and is immediately earned income for sellers.

Also, remember to make sure that all of the seller's representations about the property and the properties condition are in writing in your option and purchase contracts. The courts do not enforce oral contracts for the sale of real estate, or oral representations about real estate. All contracts regarding the sale of real estate must be in writing, or they are probably unenforceable. So, if a seller or real estate agent says he / she knows the "plumbing is in great shape" or they know for sure that the fixtures in the bathroom are "solid gold", make sure that their statement of these facts are in writing in your contracts for the options, purchase or sale of real estate.

REZONING: Getting the city or county building department to change the allowable use for a property. (Example: 1. Getting a residential house changed from residential use for a family living, to commercial use as an office, or 2. getting vacant land designated for single family homes to a zoning designation for apartments).

CHAPTER 3

REZONING RICHES

Imagine making obscene profits on real estate without building, without subdividing, without architects, without remodeling, and without construction headaches. You can use this technique of rezoning properties to make hundreds of thousands of dollars, merely by requesting and getting a zoning change. The change you request should be to a zoning category that is more expensive and in greater demand than the current zoning designation for that particular property. For instance you find a residential house for sale that is near the border of a commercial area. The house is for sale for $200,000.00 and is 2000 square feet, this is exactly $100.00 per square foot, but the nearby commercial property is in demand, and selling for $250.00 per square foot. If you can get the zoning changed from residential to commercial you will increase the value of the property from $200,000.00 dollars to $500,000.00 merely by spending anywhere from several hundred dollars to a couple of thousand dollars on a rezoning application.

Keep your rezoning intentions a secret from the sellers. Don't tell them you plan on rezoning for profit or they will simply do it themselves and keep the money. If you are a licensed real estate professional you will have no choice, because of your duty to disclose, and your inability to earn a secret profit. But, zoning changes can suddenly make the property much more valuable.

You will need to write a purchase contract with the most favorable terms you can get, or simply tender an option contract with the most favorable terms you can get. Make sure that the purchase /option contract has an inspection period giving you enough opportunity to investigate the property, or use an option contract to purchase the property with an option period long enough to see if it is feasible to get the property rezoned. In the above scenario you could make $300,000.00 dollars without hammering a nail, without decorating, without getting a building permit, without reconstruction, and without dealing with contractors. You will profit almost without effort through property rezoning.

In another scenario you find that a residential lot that is zoned R-1 (Residential Single Family) for $50,000.00, but you find that the value would triple to $150,000.00 if you could get city or county to rezone to R-8 (4 plex – 8 plex). If you purchase the property, you the landowner could then build an 8 unit apartment complex or 2 (two) four-plex units. You would make $100,000.00 dollars without building, if you can get the zoning changed from R-1 to R-8. After you change the zoning, you could relist the property for $150,000.00 as an R-8 multiunit buildable lot.

You should study the areas around the property you are considering and find out what type of property or zoning are in demand. If you are success in finding a property with rezoning potential you could make money without the hassle and expense of physically developing the property.

CHAPTER 4 **HOW TO PLANT A MONEY TREE**

...It works like this; you find a large parcel from ten to one hundred acres and subdivide it into as many buildable parcels as possible. Example: You buy 100 Acres for $100,000.00 dollars and subdivide the land and create one hundred, one acre home sites. You then hire an experienced civil engineer who is licensed in that state. You have the engineer draw up a potential parcel map for the 100 paper lots, and file it with the county assessor. Shop around for the best cost; you should pay him or her $2500.00 - $10,000.00 more or less. You then list on the all 100 properties with a broker on the MLS for $11,000.00 dollars per property. Congratulations you have just created a 1 million dollar real estate money tree. If you have to get the property financed, you can arrange with the lender to release each parcel you sell after paying a fractional part of the mortgage. In the above example you owe the bank $100,000.00 total or $1,000.00 per parcel or lot. You then arrange a "release clause" in the master mortgage or trust deed to allow partial releases of parcels as they are sold. The release clause will allow that every time you pay off, $1000.00 toward the balance due the finance company or bank, they will release 1 parcel. In this way you still are making $10,000.00 per lot after paying the bank to release each parcel individually over the course of loan as you sell lots. 100 Parcels X $10,000.00 = 1 Million Dollars that will pay dividends over and over again as a passive investment. You will make a Million Dollars or more in this scenario. Over the years these lots will gradually sell one by one and gradually increase in value. The fruit that will drop off your money tree will be $10,000.00 in cash profits for each parcel sold. If the original property is smaller, you can have the property divided into as many lots allowed for a parcel that size. A city lot is about 5000 square feet and one acre is 43,560 square feet. If you divide 43,560 by 5000 square feet this equals about 8 lots. You might want to make the parcels larger and therefore more desirable for homebuilders. If you buy a $100,000.00 25 acre sub dividable parcel you could cut it up into100 X ¼ (one quarter) acre lots and sell them for $11,000.00 and get the same result of one million dollars in profit. One quarter acre to one acre is large enough for people to build custom homes. The appreciation and acceptance of your development will be more rapid if you choose to build a home or two on any of the lots yourself. If you subdivide the property using this scenario and build a custom home on one or more of the lots. The value for all the other lots in your subdivision are established and in most cases increased dramatically. You will probably want to add some deed restrictions to maintain the value of your development. For instance you might want to allow only homes over 1500 square feet, so that someone does not decide to build a tiny 500 square foot home that then becomes an eyesore. Not only will this type of house be an eyesore, but it will decrease the value of the other lots because a small 500 square foot houses value would become a comparable value in the community. Appraisers will then have to include it on appraisals for all the other properties, which is highly undesirable. You might also include deed restrictions such no commercial activity. Most developments develop a set of CC&R's (Covenants

Conditions and Restrictions) to preclude all kinds of undesirable activities. CC & R's help maintain property value by assuring people buying into the development that they don't have to worry about eyesores or other undesirable activities that will devalue their investment. CC & R's cover things like junk cars in the driveway, no parking on the lawns, no oil dripping from vehicles, no vehicle repair work in the driveway. Sometimes even the color of paint and type of curtains is covered in CCR's. In some ways this can become too restrictive, but most of the times well thought out restrictions work to secure you money tree, and make sure that it continues to produce over the years. This technique can be used anywhere in America, but is easier to use in the southern states because of the presence of many "on site homebuilders" companies. Also, the sheer massive amounts of land available cheap in southern and rural communities benefit this type of strategy. You will encounter less regulations and red tape concerning subdivisions in rural areas. The definition of an onsite homebuilder is a builder or construction company that will finance a home and build it on your parcel if you own the parcel outright. Usually they require that the property be at least 1 acre or more, in order to secure the loan. The builder either provides or helps the owner of the property get the mortgage to pay for the construction of the landowner's home. These types of builders allow people with little cash, little credit, no credit or marginal credit; to get a home built on their land.

You can still do a money tree in urban areas, just be prepared to spend more money and do more paperwork to split the lots into a subdivision. Remember that cities have much more paperwork, cost, more building code requirements and more restrictions than county and country lots.

Your money tree once created will continue to bear fruit year after year by design. Your plan once in place frees you to relax and enjoy the best things in life, while the fruit of your labor continually drops in your lap.

CHAPTER 5

UNLICENSED REALTY DEALERSHIPS ...It is often said in the real estate business that real estate agents / brokers can make a living off real estate, but real estate investors and dealers make a killing off real estate. As a licensed real estate agent I lost many opportunities in which I could have profited. If only I had been an unlicensed real estate dealer. While working as a licensed realty agent and broker, I came across a couple struggling to make mortgage payments; they were financially strapped after the husband was laid off work. Their mortgage on their house was about $165,000.00 and they wanted to sell for $185,000.00 just to get out from under the mortgage. They had planned on taking $20,000.00 net profit and they were going to put the $20,000.00 profit in the bank and find a rental home until the job market got better. I saw their For Sale by Owner (FSBO) classified advertisement in the local Newspaper; I was a new agent with Century 21 Real Estate. I met with the couple, and after I did the research on comparable homes, I found their house had appreciated greatly in 4- 5 years, and was worth

$380,000.00. I was excited and hoped they would sell the property to me and I could make roughly $200,000.00 by buying their distressed home. They had no idea that their house had appreciated that much or that they now had roughly $200,000.00 equity, but as an agent, I had to disclose to them that their home was worth a lot more. When I told them the true value of their home, they said, "we have changed our mind, we don't want to sell for $185,000.00 now, we want to sell for $380,000.00." They wanted to naturally take advantage of the appreciated market value. So, because I was a licensed agent I had to tell them how much I was going to make if they sold to me. As a licensee I was bound by the law of agency and could not make a secret profit. This is why I feel the only advantage of being an agent / broker is that you get information on how to make money in real estate and a 3%-6% commission. But, the downside is you miss a lot of opportunities through mandatory disclosures required by law. As an unlicensed real estate dealer I could have purchased the above property, without disclosure. As an unlicensed investor I would have been able to realize the $200,000.00 dollars profit instead of losing it because of my obligation to disclose all facts to the sellers as a licensed agent. Anyone who is thinking of becoming a real estate dealer should take some real estate courses at your local community college or any reputable real estate school, then incorporate, and start your own realty investment dealership. Conversely, you also could first decide to become a licensed agent, in order to get experience. After your license expires you then could go into real estate investing. You would then enjoy the advantages and contacts from your work as a licensed agent. Being an agent for a few years will give you the inside track, knowledge and connections you need to become successful in real estate investing and some monetary commissions. Although, you could learn the same things by taking the courses and buying a selling a few homes as an investor / dealer. Any training and experience will definitely help accelerate your growth and give you significant insight. As an agent or student you would learn the vocabulary necessary to interface with buyers, sellers, agents, brokers, title companies, mortgage companies, escrow officers and others involved in the real estate business. You could even work as a part time agent and keep your current job. It is a matter of personal choice how you decide to get the knowledge and skillset to become a real estate dealer. Real estate agency and broker exams are learning tools themselves and can help you advance your knowledge. As an agent or real estate dealer, you could use option contracts to create an inventory by spending about $5000.00 in cash and buy 3-5 options on various interesting properties (read chapter 2 Controlling Thousands for Pennies). As an unlicensed dealer you could "tie up" the properties with option contracts and place all the properties up for sale in a classified newspaper advertisement. As a licensed agent you also could list your options with an agent on the MLS. Real estate professionals and investment professionals use this technique to create an inventory of listings that they control. This way they don't have to spend time and energy competing for listings in the community. This strategy makes it easy for a dealer to control their own profits, and set their own pace.

"If you have faith as small as a mustard seed,

you can say to this mulberry tree, 'Be uprooted

and planted in the sea,' and it will obey you.

(St. Luke 17:6 Holy Bible NIV)

CHAPTER 6

BECOME A CASH FLOW KING / QUEEN

...Somebody once told me that "money talks, but cash swears". If you want to live like a millionaire without having a million dollars all you need to do is create enough cash flow, so you can live rich. If you look at the upper 10% of income earners such as executives, congressmen, and professionals, the thing that sets them apart from the common people and middle class is their upper income salary. The people who are not rich, but who live rich make $100,000.00 per year or more. In other words those who have cash flow monthly of $8,333.33 per month are considered rich people in America. These are the people who can afford a good mortgage, have good credit, and have good health insurance and live above the rest of the commoners. They are not cash in the bank rich, they are cash flow rich.

In real estate it is relatively easy to become cash flow rich and if you don't become rich, at least you can live rich off your cash flow.

You become cash flow rich in several ways, using rental income property for cash flow. Rental income is passive income that you don't have to go out and work for every day. It is this passive type of income that works without you having to get up in the morning and go to a job. Imagine what it would be like if you created a cash flow income to put $8,333.33 in your pocket every month. And that $8,333.33 would come into your bank account month in and month out without you having to go to a job. You could go play golf, go to the mall, go on a picnic, or not even get out of bed and still make $100,000.00 annual income. Income which is shielded from some income taxes because of the depreciation and tax deductions for real estate ownership. Passive income in this quantity will give you financial independence and financial freedom.

You could build Five (5) 2 Bedroom duplexes (ten units) and rent them out for $833.00 per month. You could buy a 2 (two) 2 Bedroom 2 bath five-plex units (ten units) and rent them $833.00 per month. Or you could buy a 10 unit apartment complex and rent each unit out for $833.00 per month. Alternatively you could build or buy a 20 unit apartment with 1 (one) bedroom each that rent for $416.50 per month. Of course you would have the expense of acquisition, but this should help you get the picture. It does not matter how your create it, cash flow of $8,333.33 would give you financial independence and make you a cash flow king or queen. Of course $8,333.00 is not the income ceiling it is just the beginning.

CHAPTER 7 **NO BANK QUALIFICATION DEALS**

...Most people think that they have to fill out an application and qualify with a bank in order to buy and own real estate. They think that they have to have excellent credit in order to buy real estate, but this is actually not true. In fact you could be in bankruptcy and have no job or income, and still buy a house, land, and apartment complex or a business. All you need to really buy real estate is not just to try to find a house, but try to find a situation.

People with situations are anxious to sell creatively and do so every day. You can call people from FSBO (For Sale by Owner) advertisements out of the local daily newspaper or run a classified advertisement (see chapter 12 sample of real estate wanted advertisements) letting sellers know that you want to buy distressed houses and fixer uppers. You can also put up signs and pass out handbills stating you buy houses as a private investor. Letting prospects know that you can close quickly, and you would consider taking over their payments. Most distressed sellers are not looking for all cash; they are looking for "walk away money". A company I worked for bought a 3 bed 2 bath 2 car garage home in a California suburb for $1000.00 walk away cash. We had to catch up the payments (2 payments of $2,200 each = $4,400.00) and remodel the home. But, all it took was $1,000.00 Cash and looming foreclosure for that family to walk away from their house. Many distressed property owners have little equity, no equity, or sometimes negative equity (they owe more than the house is worth). However; these are all situations where you can make money for yourself if you are creative. You can create equity by improving the property. $70,000.00 worth of equity was created with carpets, paint inside and out and yard work $3,000.00. Total investment $7,400.00 created a total profit $70,000.00. There are many homeowners, investors, realtors, who have properties they would love to sell quickly. It is you job as an investor and entrepreneur to find them and offer them a solution to their problem. Many people with distressed properties or distressed situations want to save their credit, and they know a foreclosure will ruin their credit for up to 7 years, so they have a strong motivation to let someone "take over their payments" and assume their mortgage.

A distressed seller could be someone behind on their home payments. A distressed seller could be someone who must move to another state because of a sick relative, a divorce or job moves forcing them to leave the area. Your job as an investor is to find out what the sellers motivation is. Then figure out a way to satisfy their need and alleviate a stressful financial situation. With a distressed property the seller may be behind 2 (two) or 3 (three) mortgage payments and they can't catch it up. If you don't offer them a solution, they will soon lose their home, their credit, their equity, and have no money to move anyway. You as an investor could offer to catch up the payments and take over the mortgage(s) on the property and give the sellers a few thousand dollars to find a rental and move out. You can do this without bank qualification, because the seller is the bank. You have done them a favor, when you help them leave with cash instead of nothing. You gave them a solution when you helped them avoid foreclosure and save their credit.

That's how it works, you find a seller in trouble with the mortgage, who wants to sell their property. You offer them some cash in exchange for letting you take over their payments. Your main job as an investor is to find out exactly what the minimum amount of "walking money" it is going to take to induce the seller to let you take over their payments.

Distressed sellers usually don't require an application, don't require income verification, don't require anything other than a certain amount of cash that they need to walk away. If you have good, fair, or bad credit, they won't know if you don't tell them. They are in distressed and they are not a bank, so if they can get enough cash to leave and have a reasonable assurance you will keep making the payments, they are happy to take the cash and go.

For Example: You find a property 124 Bluebird Lane, Newtown, Chicago and find out that
the people selling want to leave Chicago and move back to Kansas, where their mother and
father are old and in need of care.

They may need $5,000.00 to pay movers and for travel money to get back to Kansas, and for this amount, they would let someone else assume their house and mortgage payments. You draw up a purchase contract for their home, and the seller owes $350,000.00 to BIG BANCORP. The contract will state that you will pay them $5,000.00 Cash to assume the payments "Subject To" the existing $350,000.00 Loan to BIG BANCORP Bank. They hand you a notarized Grant Deed deeding the property to you or your company. You then record you deed with a title company or county recorder, recording your interest in the property. Always assume properties and mortgages with the stipulation in writing that the assumption is "SUBJECT TO" the existing financing. The reason for this is that the "Subject To" wording will in most states protect you financially. If you were just to use the words "ASSUMPTION" or "ASSUME" the existing mortgages, this would make you personally responsible to the bank who owns the mortgages assumed. The words assume "SUBJECT TO" keeps the original borrower responsible to the bank. So, a word to the wise always use the words

"SUBJECT TO" when assuming a property. If you are the seller and you were selling you would want to use the only the word "ASSUMPTION" to pass the mortgage responsibility on to the buyer.

I usually make sure any distressed sellers have moved all their furniture and clothing out of the house, before giving them the final money payment, in order to make sure they don't end up being a renter, or a holdover, which could mean I would have to evict them, which could be costly, frustrating and time consuming.

"A half a loaf of bread, is better than none"
(An Idiom)

CHAPTER 8

MAKING MONEY WITH EQUITY SHARES

...Equity Sharing is about owning property with another investor. Usually, people partner or do equity sharing because they don't have the credit or money to buy the desired property by themselves. The potential buyer finds a person with credit and money to partner with, and goes half on ownership. They purchase the property as a team. Usually one party and agrees to live in or manage the property, and make the mortgage payments and the other party puts up the credit and money. Both partners share the tax benefits and appreciation. They could both live in it and share the expenses also. But at a future predetermined time usually 2-5 years, one team member buyer will purchase the property from the partnership, or the property is will be offered for sale on the open market through a realtor or agent. When the property is sold the two will share the profits and other benefits of the sale. The key to equity sharing is finding and meeting both parties' needs thorough the division of the responsibilities and benefits of ownership. They share the resources and costs necessary to acquire real estate and maintain it, and the benefits of ownership. These responsibilities and benefits are divided ahead of time by contract to assure that both parties are receiving an agreeable share of both responsibilities and benefits of the ownership of the property.

Most people assume that equity share ownership is always 50% / 50% but this is not always the case. In equity sharing you can have uneven ownership 60% / 40%, 30% / 70% and even 90% / 10%. Also, you can have uneven distribution of tax benefits.

The person who need the tax shelter more than the money, could own 75% of the tax advantages, And the other party could own 25% of the tax advantages. Or in another scenario one person could be responsible for 100% of the mortgage while receiving only 50% of the tax advantages.
Also, you can share income from the property, for example partner A receives 30%
The income, while partner B receives 70% of the income.

As you can see people involved in investing in equity share real estate have some different and some of the same goals. Some investors are seeking income, some are seeking tax savings, and some are seeking merely participation as a passive investment. Whatever two or more people decide as the agreed upon goal can be the basis for a shared equity agreement in real estate.

For example, if two people buy a home together with market value of $500,000.00 dollars and agree to hold the property for 5 years and sell for future market value. Both parties are hoping that the property will be worth $650,000.00 and they will split the $150,000.00 appreciation between them, using the predetermined equity split formula. In the above scenario the $150,000.00 appreciation is to be divided at the sale or re-finance of the property which would complete the agreement. If it a 33% for the Party A and a 66% and

Party B will receive 33 % then party A will receive approx. $100,000.00 Cash and Party B will receive

Approx. $50,000.00 at the end of 5 years. If during the course of the agreement over the 5 year period tax benefits are $100,000.00 and the tax benefits split is 50% / 50% then the both parties will write off $10,000.00 each for 5 years on their income tax.

Equity Sharing is a great way to get started for a person with limited credit and limited cash for a down payment. However; there are things that can go wrong. If the property value goes down, and then there is no equity to divide. Let's say that the value goes down from $500,000.00 to $400,000.00 there must be provisions in the agreement to determine how the $100,000.00 negative equity (the loss) will be split, or how long the equity share agreement will be extended In order to allow the market value to go back up or surpass the original sales price. In theory however; the price of real estate rarely goes down, however; it is possible for the value to fall and create a problem for the equity share team.

"For nothing is impossible with God."
(Luke 1:37 Holy Bible)

CHAPTER 9

DON'T FLIP HOUSES – CONTROL FLIP

...Most people have heard of real estate flippers, who buy a property in January for $175,000.00 and sell it in February for $250,000.00 for a quick $75,000.00 profit. That is an example of a real estate flip. In a controlled flip another investor has already agreed to buy the property for more money that the purchase price. This is an example of a controlled flip. The team agrees that after certain improvements are made by the original Investor, the property will be sold to a partner investor with a markup profit. The key to this concept is in the name CONTROL! If two parties agree to prosper together, and split the profits, this is an optimum situation. As long as the profits are sufficient and lucrative enough to satisfy both parties, the two can buy and sell pre-arranged agreed upon properties and split the profits between themselves anyway they want. One optimal situation is a builder who builds income duplexes, tri-plexes, four-plexes and apartments, and then finds a person who will be the end owner after construction. The means the property is not built on "spec" (speculation), it is built on a guarantee that it will be purchased. The property ownership and profits can be split and shared anyway the control flippers want, in order to optimize their investment profits.

Suppose two investors Dan and Willie decide that they want to split 1 million dollars in 5 Real estate transactions, then Dan would go out and buy 10 properties for $250,000.00 remodel them and add value to them and Sell all them to Willie for $350,000.00, every deal would create a $100,000.00 profit on per transaction. The 10 (Ten) Properties at $100,000.00 profit for Dan would equal 1 Million Dollars. He could simple convey $50,000.00 Cash/Equity after each transaction, during the 10 transactions. Dan would have then have $500,000.00 (half a million dollars) and Willie would have $500,000.00 (half a million Dollars). They could then cease operations or they could choose to continue flipping. They can continue as long as they were still able to maintain the real estate, payments and rent or sell off the units.

Another way to control flip which is also lucrative is to be an owner builder and end user purchase team. One party could build and sell to the other. Dan can borrow $500,000.00 to build a 1 .5 Million dollar income property (apartments) to sell to Willie who is a guaranteed buyer. If a builder does not have to worry about selling the property he is constructing, he is guaranteed a nice profit and it is much easier to get financing. If he shares that profit with the seller, most banks would probably have an issue with it, if the bank knew of the arrangement. Banks don't like these types of arrangements; they are considered non-arm's length transactions, some private money lenders are less stringent on these types of arrangements or don't care. Check with your realtor or mortgage lender as to their institutional policy.

CHAPTER 10

CREATE YOUR OWN PRIVATE BANK

...If you have good credit you will not have a lot of obstacles to real estate investing, because of your ability to borrow at low interest rate from banks. However; if you don't have good credit you will probably not be able to qualify for a bank loan, or if you do qualify it will be at very high interest rates and the mortgage may have a balloon payment that could come due (pop) on you. Some industry professionals say that "Balloon Payments are for clowns". However; Balloon payments used properly can make you a lot of money if you can get it correctly. Also, even if you are credit challenged you can still borrow a lot of money by creating your own financial system. All you need to do is advertise for investors and have some sales ability. This step requires some upfront money for you to pay for local advertisements in newspapers in the finance section. Usually there is money wanted section, or business investments section in the local daily newspapers with a large circulation. This is the optimum place where you want to place advertisements asking for investor capital. Here are a couple of examples, but the key is to look at other long running advertisements for "money wanted" to see what is actually working for others that are already in the newspaper. Then model your advertisement after the advertisements that you see continuously. If you see an advertisement of any type that runs in the paper over and over again, it is a sign that the advertisement is successfully producing results. All you have to do is clone (copy) the advertisement and change a few things to make it fit your situation. One of the keys to advertisement is to make sure the newspaper circulation is large. I personally prefer advertising in newspapers with over 1 million distribution. Numbers play a large part in the success of any advertising campaign, and real estate advertisements are no different. Sometimes small publications can be profitable also, but as a rule try for the largest distribution circulation you can afford.

SAMPLE MONEY WANTED

CLASSIFIED ADVERTISMENTS

EXAMPLE #1

$10,000.00 returns $15,000.00 in 180 days

Secured by Real Estate Call Dan 555-555-5555

EXAMPLE #2

$25,000.00 need for 1 Year, returns 10% interest

Secured by Real Estate Call Dan 555-555-5555

EXAMPLE #3

$50,000.00 for 1 year Secured by 2nd Deed of Trust

12% int. Residential Home Call Dan 555-555-5555

EXAMPLE #4

$100,000.00 Construction Loan 15% interest

1 Year secured by real estate Call 555-555-5555

CHAPTER 11

HOW TO BUY FIXER UPPERS CHEAP

...One of the main things you should know is how to

acquire fixer uppers. For an investor it is the

 key that will help you acquire inventory. The best

way to acquire inventory passively is to

review the daily paper in your area for properties for

sale in the area and price range you want

to buy houses.   This would entail a daily search

mainly looking for "FSBOs" (for sale by owner

properties). For sale by owner and properties owned

by real agents and broker are good sources

for creative financing, because the properties listed

are usually listed by people who know how to

creatively transfer title. Credit is usually a minor or

no consideration in creatively financed properties.

Real estate agents and brokers acquire properties

through the normal course of business and

sometimes themselves are in possession of a

property that is costing them too much for mortgage

payments and upkeep. These properties owned by

real estate agents and brokers are usually easy to

acquire, fix and repair. They are easier to acquire because, the agent is very experts on how to transfer title and don't need to be taught as much as some other non-licensed FSBO's. But, the best way to acquire properties aggressively is to run an advertisement in the real estate wanted section.

When most people think about fixer uppers they think that it will cost them a lot of money for a down payment, and then they will need to spend tens of thousands of dollars fixing the property up. If you use the techniques in this book, you will be able to put only a little cash down and not have to worry about income and credit qualifications. The key is that you must come to understand the motivation of people who want to sell a home that is distressed or badly in need of repair. First of all if a home is really ugly it does not mean that the house is not structurally sound. The house may have bad paint, ugly yard, and horrid old wall paper and maybe some holes in the walls, but still have a strong, foundation, wall system, good electrical, and a good roof.

The seller of an ugly house or distressed property, are motivated because he or she knows that the house is a mess and needs beautification. The seller has probably talked to many potential buyers who were resistant to the ugly property, and the seller needs to get the property sold and make some money in the process. The seller of an ugly house is usually reasonable about down payment, and flexible about financing, which is what you want.

You as an investor want to make an offer to purchase the home with little money down and offer to take over the payments. You can ask the seller to do a wraparound loan on the property. A wrap around is a creative financing technique that does not require a new bank loan and the seller can act as the bank. Make sure if you choose to do a wraparound mortgage that the bank gets their portion of any payments every month, so the property does not go into foreclosure, while you are working to improve the property. You cannot rely on the seller to make the payments to the bank, because they may neglect to make the payments.

One way to assure the seller and help the seller assure themselves that payments will be made on the property is to use a "note servicing company." Such as www.meracord.com   (formerly known as Note World) or some other similar payment processing company.

Also, before making a down payment and getting into contract with the seller, make sure that the seller is current on the payments or the transaction includes provisions to make up back payments. Ask a local title company to do a title search on the property. You can also ask the seller for the most current mortgage statement from the bank. This way you can avoid getting stuck with payments that are behind, but not disclosed by the seller. Sellers may say that all payments are current, but this must be verified so you don't have an unexpected expense.

There are some properties you should steer clear of as a new investor. Such as properties that need major repairs like a new roof, new electrical system, new plumbing, condemned buildings or building that have foundation problems. These problems are too costly, complicated and may make the investments not worthwhile for new investors. Unless of course you are an electrician buying a house that needs new electrical, or a plumber buying a house that needs new plumbing. If you are a roofer and the house needs a new roof, because that house may be a good investment. However; to the person who knows nothing about roofing, it is definitely a bad investment.

Major structural problems can be avoided by paying a property inspector $150 - $250.00 to do a professional report. Pest control is usually a minor consideration in most cases, but it depends on the kind of pest. The cost of the pest control can be known in advance of purchasing the property through a recommended pest control report. At any rate you must do your own due diligence in any situation and know exactly what you are getting into and the approximate costs of repairing any problems.

Once you get possession and ownership of the property through and assumption, wrap around mortgage, seller carry of the sale, or new mortgage financing, it is time to go to work fixing up the property. One common mistake of inexperienced real estate investors is to overspend money on major changes on the property. Remember, you are trying to resell the property so keeping the cost of fix up low is a way to make the property more competitively priced, and increasing the amount of profits for you when the property is sold. If you as an investor put in a $25,000.00 swimming pool, you will only be able to recover about $5,000.00 from that large capital investment in the property. Swimming pools are the best value when you buy them already installed at the property. It is an investors rule that you make greater profits off cosmetic work, like carpets, linoleum paints, yard work, countertops and new appliances. Cosmetic work pays greater profit dividends than major work on the property. Adding a room for instance may cost $25,000.00 - $30,000.00 but only add $25,000.00 - $30,000.00 to the sale price, which is a waste of time. In general large structural expenditures negatively affect resale profits, and small cosmetic expenditures positively affect the resale profits of the sale.

Keep in mind that you are fixing up the house for sale, not to keep. Another mistake is using the most expensive paint, the most expensive flooring, the most expensive fixtures, thinking this will bring much greater fix up rewards, but generally this is not true. A good rule of thumb is you don't use the lowest quality and don't use the highest quality. Instead use a good general quality. Using the lowest quality sometimes will have the reverse effect on profits. The very cheap fixtures will look very cheap and not create the desire to own by buyers looking for a home. However; a good general quality is usually appreciated by all, and does not cost much more that the low quality. The good general quality is much lower cost than the top quality. So, be careful not to over pay for Improvements and be sure to keep costs low.

If you are not going to do the work yourself, try

to find someone with good skills that does

not charge outrageous prices for services.

Remember, when you save $1,000.00 dollars it adds

$1,000.00 to your potential profit. When you find

someone that does a good job for you and

That does work at very reasonable prices, cultivate

that relationship and use these artisans over

and over again. I have personally had bids on work

of $50,000.00 and got the work completed

with material for under $5,000.00. This gave me an

additional $45,000.00 potential profit at

the sale of the property.

I use to make a practice painting all my fixer

uppers inside myself using all contractors white,

which made painting a whole lot easier. I would

merely cover the floor if I was keeping the flooring,

or rip out the flooring if I was replacing the flooring

and cover the appliances with plastic or newspaper.

And I would buy a cheap $125.00 paint sprayer

from a hardware store and buy several 5 gallon cans

of contractor eggshell white paint. I would then hire my son for $300.00 per day and he would paint the entire interior while I assisted or worked on other areas of the house. I would usually find a professional painter for the outside to improve curb appeal. Unless you are a professional painter, hire a paint contractor for the outside at least. It will improve the value much more than a unprofessional outside paint job. Curb appeal is everything when selling a house.

When you are ready to sell the property after fix up, try selling the property yourself instead of using a real estate agent. It is easy to open an escrow with a title company. The escrow officer will guide you through the transaction anyway. Escrow officers won't charge you a commission, because the escrow fee is their pay. You will save the 5%-6% real estate commission which is usually tens of thousands of dollars and this savings will translate into additional profit on your fixer upper project.

Agents are great, but a good title company is usually the best option to process any sales and transfer of the property title. Sometimes title companies are unwilling to process a real estate transaction without notifying the bank of record on an existing mortgage if there is no new loan. The title companies do not want the bank coming back to to sue them over any "due on sale clause" or "acceleration clause" in the mortgage.

Unless you have a lot of experience transferring titles to real estate, it is almost always advisable to use an agent or title company, and pay the usually reasonable escrow fee and a policy of title insurance. Title insurance will make it easier to sell the property when you are ready to sell, because title insurance guarantees that you will not have problems with title issues. Title issues may make it difficult to impossible to sell the property. Title insurance will insure your interest in the property for problems that happened before you took possession. Such as someone who forgot to record a deed or recorded a deed incorrectly, as well as unknown liens.

If you are a real estate professional and you cannot find a title company to help you, seek out a real estate attorney and pay them for a 1 (one) hour consultation. If you have done a lot of real estate deals in the past, you can sometimes do your own research and have the seller "Grant Deed" the property to you directly, through a Notary Public and record the deed with the appropriate city or county recorder. This will negate the need of going through the formal escrow process.

If you have never done a real estate transaction before, you should use a real estate agent on the first 1 or 2 deals or at the very least a use a reputable title company. A title company is less expensive that real estate agents. If you are really unsure, use an agent or broker on your first few transactions. After you get some experience you can just open an escrow yourself through a title company and skip paying thousands in commission to a real estate brokerage.

On the next page you will find some sample advertisements for you to run in the local newspaper in the classified section. You will get lots of calls and you should have a list of questions ready. Some sample questions are listed after the sample advertisements on page 87.   You can use these questions as a base, and you should come up with a few of your own questions. The question you ask should depend on your investment goals. For instance if you are only buying home with a large yard, one of your questions should be "How big is the lot the home is on?" And if you are looking only at home that is a lite fixer, one of your questions should be "Does the home have any major problems?"

FIXER UPPER AQUISTION ADVERTISMENTS

Example #1

TOP CASH FOR HOUSES

Hassel Free! Quick Close!

Call James 555-555-5555

Example #2

CASH FOR YOUR HOUSE!

Any condition, any price

Call James 555-555-5555

Example #3

NEED TO SELL FAST?

We specialize in distressed situations

Call James 555-555-5555

Example #4

WE BUY FIXER UPPERS

Ugly houses that need work wanted

Call James 555-555-5555

FIXXER UPPER PURCHASE QUESTIONS

INCOMING CALLS FROM HOME SELLERS

1. What is the property address?

2. How many bedrooms and baths?

3. How much are you asking for the home?

4. How much cash do you need down?

5. Why are you selling?

6. How long have you had it on the market?

7. What condition is the home in?

8. When can I see the home?

9. Is the home listed with an agent of broker?

10. Do you have any offers on the home?

11. Do you currently live in the home?

12. If so how soon could you move out?

13. _____?

14. _____?

15. _____?

Note: You don't need to ask all these questions, on the pertinent ones. Some of them may get answered before you can ask. So, be patient and pleasant and smile into the phone and be polite at all times!

FIXER UPPER SALES

CLASSIFIED ADVERTISMENTS

Example #1

STARTER HOUSE FOR SALE

Possible Seller Carry or Low Down Payment

Owner 555-555-5555

Example #2

NEWLY REMODELED HOME

New Paint, New Carpets Needs New Owner

Call Owner 555-555-5555

Example #3

FIRST TIME HOMEBUYERS WELCOME!

We can help get you qualified.

Call Seller /Owner 555-555-5555

Example #4

HOUSE SEEKING FAMILY!

All the work is done, must see! EZ Terms!

Call Owner 555-555-5555

But without faith it is impossible to please him:

(Hebrews 11:6 KJV)

CHAPTER 12

BIG BUCKS AS AN OWNER BUILDER

...Some people think you need to be a contractor to build a house, but this is not true. Contactors charge the public about 35% above the actual cost of building a house as a profit margin for supervising other people's construction. If you become an owner builder, you can claim the 35% as profit for yourself. You cannot contract to build a house for other people in most states, as an owner builder. You can however, sell the houses or apartments you build after they are constructed. The difference is in states that require licensing for contractors; licensed contractors can solicit business from the public, whereas you cannot as a non-licensed person.

Here is how it works. You find a piece of land that is buildable and zoned for residential / commercial construction. You take out a construction loan, which by arrangement with the bank will get incremental construction draws. Remember, when you set up the construction loan you and the bank decides when the draws will take place. Usually, there is an immediate draw after loan closing and 5 – 7 draws at different phases of completion. The key is to spend less than the draw allows for and keeps the rest as income or profit as your own general contractor. For instance, if the construction draw allows for $20,000.00 for the foundation work and you are able to get the job completed for $15,000.00, then you will get to keep the $5,000.00 at that stage of development. If the framing allows for a $35,000.00 draw and you are able to get all the framing done for $25,000.00 then you will keep the $10,000.00 for acting as your own general contractor / owner builder. You can use a new construction purchase agreement to purchase property, if you know what type of structure you will be building on the land. In essence the seller is selling you the property with the agreement that you are going to build a house on the land. Some lenders fund construction loans that are based on the future value of the property. If you have a property that is now worth $500,000.00 but will be worth 1.5 million after improving the existing structure. The lender will make the loan based on the value of 1.5 million. This gives the borrower greater borrowing power. In this example the lender loans money at a 75% loan to value rate, in this situation he will loan a maximum of 1 million to improve the subject property.

First you will have to hire an appraiser to do a projection appraisal, based on the land, the location and the type of structure you are building. The appraiser treats the appraisal the same as any other appraisal except for the fact that the construction is not complete but anticipated. The value is based on what the property will be worth after the building and improvements are completed. The appraiser uses comparable properties, location, and square footage to determine what a property will be worth after it is built. In this way it assures the lender that after they loan you money to construct a building, it will be worth a certain amount of money as collateral after the construction is complete.

You may have a piece of buildable land you purchased for $10,000.00 and want to build a duplex on the land. You know that construction will cost will be $50,000.00 and permits and other will cost you another $15,000.00 for a total cost of $65,000.00. You get an appraiser to calculate from your duplex building plan the dimensions, bedrooms, baths, etc. If the appraiser comes up with a value of $150,000.00 at the completion of the construction. The construction lender will fund the construction based on a percentage of the $150,000.00 completion value, also known as a LTV (Loan to Value) ratio. Here is a table based on this particular scenario.

LOAN TO VALUE CHART:

EXAMPLE

VALUE	LOAN TO VALUE	LOAN AMOUNT
$150,000.00 X	50%	= $75,000.00
$150,000.00 X	60%	= $90,000.00
$150,000.00 X	70%	= $105,000.00
$150,000.00 X	80%	= $120,000.00
$150,000.00 X	90%	= $135,000.00
$150,000.00 X	100%	= $150,000.00

So, if a bank is willing to loan you at least 50% of the final value or $75,000.00. You project is feasible, and you will be able to build the property for $65,000.00 and have $10,000.00 left over in case of unexpected expenses. Of course you will usually have to make payments, but you may be able to arrange with the lender to include the payments in the loan amount. Including payments means you are not burdened with payments during construction.

One thing that you should strongly consider is borrowing enough to definitely have excess funds, so that after every draw you have some money left over for your income or as a cash reserve. This way you can expect regular income after every phase of construction.   If you need to borrow $100,000.00 dollars, borrow $125,000.00, so if you have 5 phases of development where you need $20,000.00 each phase, you will get $25,000.00 each phase. You then can put the $5,000.00 in your pocket, or keep the money as an emergency cash reserve. At the end of construction you will have $25,000.00 cash to pay for remarketing, loan fees or other costs.

You can also can use the strategy to do home improvements construction projects. Such as, adding a room, adding a bathroom, dividing a large room into two rooms. Turning 2 Bedroom 1 Bath Homes into 3 bed 2 bath home. You can turn a 3 bedroom 1 bath homes into 3 Bedroom 2 bath homes, or turning 3 bedroom 2 bath homes into 5 bedroom 2 bath homes. The possibilities are as endless as your imagination and budget.

Suppose you purchase an older home that had 2 bedrooms and 1 Bath for $200,000.00 and you added another 2 Bedrooms and 1 bath upstairs, you will then be in possession of a 4 Bath 2 Bedroom home that is worth approximately $350,000.00. The idea is that you can create equity. Equity can be created not just by building from the ground on raw land, but by adding rooms, adding garages, adding bathrooms, enlarging the kitchen. Be creative, because the creativity in you is an asset worth a fortune.

Just minor remodeling alone creates value by itself. New paint, wallpaper, new window covering, new stove, refrigerator, new carpet, new tile, etc.

As a matter of fact if you are a beginner in real estate investing, you should only do cosmetic fixer uppers. It is too easy for you to spend   more money than you should trying to expand or build onto a property. However; if you have done construction in the past or you have family or close associates who can do the work, please use those resources. You should always let an appraiser or a licensed real estate professional determine the finished value, before you expend thousands on a room addition or bathroom addition. Make double sure that the addition will bring the added value you need, to make it worth the investment in time and money.

Also, you might consider hiring a glass patio enclosure company who can turn your patio into another bedroom. Usually, they can give you a written estimate for a glass enclosure of a patio or other space around the home, making it cost efficient and profitable to add on to the home. Check it out first though, before you sign the contract.

All things are possible to them that believe.

(St. Mark 9:23 Holy Bible)

CHAPTER 13

BUSINESS FORMATION TIPS!

It is a good idea if you are going to consider opening a part time or full time real estate Investment Company to decide on a business form in which you want to operate. If you present yourself in a professional business manner, nobody is going to want to do business with you.

#1 DECIDE ON A BUSINESS FORM:

SOLE PROPRITORSHIP / MOM AND POP

File a Fictitious Business Name with City or County

OR A CORPORATE FORM Profit Corporation (S-Corp or Regular Corp)

Partnership/Limited Partnership

Limited Liability Corporation / LLC(S-Corp or Regular)

Call Attorney or Use Cheap Web Alternatives Below:

www.corporatecreations.com

www.legalzoom.com

www.mycorporation.com

www.BizFilings.com

DECIDE WHICH STATE YOU WILL INCORPORATE IN:

SUGGESTED STATES: Delaware, Nevada, Wyoming, or the state your business will operate in.

DECIDE ON A BUSINESS NAME:

Examples: ABC Realty Investments Corp

123 Real Estate Group, Inc.

Fast Start Realty, LLC

GET INEXSPENSIVE BUSINESS CARDS:

www.iprint.com

www.vistaprint.com

www.print.staples.com

GET A BUSINESS LICENSE:

(County Clerk / City Hall / Local Government)

GET A QUICK INEXSPENSIVE WEBSITE:

www.1and1.com

www.godaddy.com

www.yahoo.com

www.register.com

www.twocows.com

www.lunarpages.com

www.squarespace.com

NOTE: If you are confused about the best type of business entity to form for your business, you should consult a tax professional or business attorney. LLC's with S-Corp Status are the most popular at this time. LLC's give you corporate protection without a lot of administrative overhead. S-Corp status usually means that each individual will only be taxed on what they make, and avoids double taxation of the corporation and then the owners. The most popular states are Wyoming and Delaware. Nevada Corporations are good, but have been stigmatized by Organized Crime elements. Nevada may still be a good choice if you realize how you will be viewed by banks, lenders, potential investors and partners. Also Nevada could be ideal if you will operate in Nevada.

CHAPTER 14 **SETTING GOALS FOR YOUR**

BUSINESS ...You should spend time thinking about what type of strategy you will have for your business successes. You should try to find the chapter or strategy in this book that you like the best. Think about what techniques you think fit your personality, business model, and financial goals. You should try to determine how much money you want to make? And what kind of money you want to make such as rental income or flip income. What type of real estate interests you? Land, Houses, Apartments, Commercial Property? Hotels, Motels, store front rentals? You should do an assessment on how much money you have to invest, how much money you need to borrow to invest. Check your credit, and see if you can improve it, with some credit clean up or repair. Decide if you will you partner with someone for cash or credit. Decide if you need and office or will you work from home, a virtual office is recommended. These things are all relevant and all these decision will affect your real estate investment business. Write down your thoughts and goals on the next page.

CHAPTER 15

NO DOWN PAYMENT WITH CASH OUT

...100 Percent financing also called No Down Payment financing with our without Cash Out is relatively easy to accomplish if the seller of the property is motivated and flexible. One common way to finance 100% of the sale price of real estate property is to get a 50% 1st loan from a lender that does not care where or how you get the other 50% down payment. Usually "Hard Money" lenders don't care where the down payment comes from, because their money is secured by the property (collateral) and your credit is only a minor consideration. It is easier to buy a property from a seller that owns outright the property being sold. This would mean that the seller did not have any outstanding mortgage loans on the subject property. **SCENARIO #1** If the property was valued at $500,000.00 you could go out and get a hard money loan for $250,000.00 (50% of Sale Price) and get the seller to carry a 2nd note for $250,000.00 (Other 50% of the Sale Price) and you would have accomplished you goal of buying a home with 100% financing with no money down. Of course you will have some escrow costs amounting to several hundred to several thousand dollars. If you wanted to achieve even greater leverage (borrowing power), and get some cash in your pocket you could use the same scenario but ask the seller to credit you some of the 1st Loan Proceeds back in escrow for repairs or costs. The seller would then carry a larger second note on the property. **SCENARIO #2** On the same $500,000.00 property you would arrange a $250,000.00 loan for the first mortgage, but ask the seller to credit you $50,000.00 through escrow if the lender allows in escrow credits. Then the seller will carry a 2nd note for $300,000.00   instead, to cover the $250,000.00 2nd, plus the $50,000.00 cash he credited you. This will allow you to finance the property 110%. **SCENARIO #3** If you want even greater cash out, you could ask the seller to credit you $100,000.00 through escrow and accomplish 120% financing. The seller would then carry a 2nd note for $350,000.00. The transaction would look like this.

If the lender does not allow in escrow credits, you would ask the seller to credit you $50,000.00 outside of escrow. The seller could give you a check that is good for $50,000.00 that you will hold pending close of escrow, or sign an unrecorded contract to give you a check for $50,000.00 after close of escrow.

SCENARIO #1   100% Financing

$1000.00 down from you for escrow fees

$250,000.00 1st Loan from Lender

$250,000.00 Seller Carry 2nd Mortgage

SCENARIO #2   100% Financing + 50K Cash

$1000.00 down from you for escrow fees

$250,000.00 1st Loan from Lender

$ - 50,000.00 Seller Credit to you the Buyer

$300,000.00 Seller Carry 2nd Mortgage

SCENARIO #3   100% Financing and 100K Cash

$1000.00 down from you for escrow fees

$250,000.00 1st Loan from Lender

$ -100,000.00 Seller Credit to you the Buyer

$350,000.00 Seller Carry 2nd Mortgage

CHAPTER 16

MAGIC CASH WITH SUBORDINATION

...In the previous chapter we discussed how you could achieve 100% to 120% financing. Subordination however is even a more potent weapon to pull even greater amounts of cash out of a property. Subordination is a powerful tool because you have the potential to borrow up to 200% of a property's value (double the value of the property). If the property was valued at $500,000.00 you could potentially borrow 1 Million Dollars on it. This is not likely, but is possible if you had the seller's formal or informal co-operation in a subordinated mortgage. Formal co-operation would mean that the seller understood the consequences of a subordination clause in seller assisted financing and does not care about the consequences. Informal seller co-operation would mean that the seller does not understand the consequences of subordination in seller assisted financing, but agrees to it in writing. As a private investor it IS NOT your job to educate other parties, it is your job to capitalize on your knowledge. If you are a licensed real estate professional you have the obligation to explain to the uneducated, but as a private investor you are not obligated to look out for the other guy. Subordination clauses are usually used when a buyer plans to build on a vacant piece of land, or a buyer plans to improve upon a property that is already built after purchasing it. And usually a seller knows and agrees that the borrower is going to be getting a construction loan and this is the reason for the subordination clause in the seller assisted mortgage. However if the seller does not understand subordination, or the sellers real estate agent does not understand subordination, then the seller may be in for a rude awakening and expensive lesson in life at worst. Because, if the seller allows a subordination clause to be place in the financing documents, the seller is giving you a way to take equity out of the property legally and borrow up to twice as much as the property is worth (200% financing). Subordination itself is not an evil concept or a good concept, it is an amoral concept. It is the way the subordination is used that makes it either good or bad. For subordination to work properly in a seller assisted transaction, the seller would have to have the property that is being sold "paid off" or close to being paid off (owe very little on it). Any other money that is owed on a property is usually paid off with the new loan on the property. If a house was valued at $400,000.00 by an appraisal and had no outstanding mortgages were on it, you could arrange to buy the property from the seller for full price or $400,000.00 (which would be attractive to seller), and give the seller a 1st Note or Mortgage instrument for $400,000.00 amortized over 10, 15, or 30 years with interest. On a 30 year note that would mean that you would repay approximately 1 Million Dollars for the $400,000.00 extension of mortgage credit by the seller (which would be attractive to seller). The seller would not have to pay capital gains on the $400,000.00 since it would be paid monthly. The seller would simply pay taxes on the amount of money received (payments) on an annual basis (which should also be attractive to seller). However; if the seller allowed you to place a subordination clause in the contract of the Note or Trust Deed, you could go out and borrow money as if the seller's $400,000.00 note did not exist. That means that the day after the close of escrow (C.O.E.), you could go out a get a 50% Loan to value mortgage in 1st place for $200,000.00 cash, and it would take precedence over the sellers original $400,000.00 mortgage even though the new loan occurred after the original sale (this would NOT be attractive to a seller). This would in effect give you 150% financing. If you were a licensed real estate professional in most states, you would have to explain to the seller the subordination clause in the original $400,000.00 mortgage would achieve an inferior status to any new money you pulled out later, because of the subordination clause in the $400,000.00 mortgage. If anything went wrong after you pulled out the additional $200,000.00 and you went into default on the loan, the seller would have to cover your $200,000.00 loan in order to protect his $400,000.00 note, and the $400,000.00 note would now only be worth a maximum of $200,000.00 because of the additional $200,000.00 you borrowed after the sale. The seller would have to pay this back out of his equity to save the property from foreclosure (NOT good for seller).   If you are a seller you usually don't want to allow someone to have a subordination clause on the property that you sell them. If you are a buyer and borrower you would very much benefit from having a subordination clause inserted into the sales contract and the mortgage security instrument or note. There are times when a subordination clause is desirable for both parties, but the reasons for using the subordination should be spelled out very carefully to protect the seller. By stating specifically in the subordination clause when a buyer can exercise subordination rights. If you allow someone to insert a subordination clause into a contract on a house that you are selling, make sure that the terms are carefully crafted to protect you. Specifically spell out what kind or loan, and how the funds have to be used to protect both parties from misunderstandings about the use of the clause and more importantly this specific use of funds from any new loan.   In a nutshell, a subordination clause in a 1st deed of trust or 1st mortgage, allows it to be treated like a 2nd deed or trust or mortgage. So, even if it is recorded 1st, it will be looked on as recorded 2nd. So, in fact the 1st loan that is subordinated is really a 2nd loan, which is waiting for someone to take out a 1st loan. This is a recipe for disaster without safeguards in place to make sure that any new funds borrowed under the subordination clause are used to increase the value of the property that is held as collateral. An unscrupulous borrower could use a subordination clause to legally strip the equity from a property, and leave the seller with a worthless mortgage and foreclosed property.

It cannot be overstated that if a subordination clause and subordination financing is used properly; it is a valuable tool for the buyer and the seller. If the subordination clause is used correctly, a buyer of vacant land, can use it to borrow enough money on the property to build a house on it. Another proper use of a subordination clause is to use any new funds to renovate and improve an existing structure. Generally speaking if the new loan is going to add value to an existing property, that is greater than the amount of the new loan, the use would be proper and desirable. See an attorney or licensed real estate agent before allowing subordination.

All hard work brings a profit, but mere talk

leads only to poverty. (The Bible Proverbs

14:23 NIV)

CHAPTER 17 CONCLUSION

...The process of becoming a successful real estate investor and entrepreneur may seem daunting. But remember that many people from all walks of life have been successful. People from every background and culture have successful bought and sold homes profitably from the beginning of the creation of this nation and even globally. Real estate has continued to increase in value since this nation began and is one of the foundations of this nation's wealth. If you will commit yourself to put in the time and energy to succeed you will become successful. Just follow the simple technics in this book, and even improve upon them and you will make money, build your own fortune, and realize your dreams. It is advisable to set up a plan of action in writing so, you will know what you want and what you want to accomplish. It does not have to be a full scale business plan, but it should be in writing. You can always adapt your plan later if you find a particular interest in real estate deals. Believe in yourself and believe in your plan, follow the examples in this book and you will become a winner like so many others before you!

MY GOALS IN REAL ESTATE INVESTING

1._____

_____

2._____

_____

3._____

_____

4._____

_____

5._____

_____

6_____

7._____

8._____

_____

9._____

_____

10._____

_____